Lady on a Wire

Poetry by
Shannon Lynette

Lady on a Wire
ISBN-13: 978-1479382378
ISBN-10: 147938237X
Copyright © 2012, Shannon Lynette

Cover Photo by Shannon Lynette
Artwork by Tina Foote
Book design and author photo by Shannon Lynette

More information on Shannon Lynette and her poetry can be found at www.facebook.com/ladyonawire and www.ladyonawire.com. You may also email her directly at ladyonawire@gmail.com.

For Lenin and Halo

Make it worth your while, live it up and live it loud

CONTENTS

I can come up with a
convenient theory to justify any
immoral situation you find yourself in.
- *Andrea Bonacci*

BURNT AMBER

Fire burns brightly
Sycamore leaves
Charcoaled sculptures
Easily erased

Paint your face with burnt amber
And dance with the bush
You torched with your tongue

Fly so high in a paper airplane
The wind dies and so do I
And maybe, just maybe
I am but never will be
Who you thought I have become

At night riding an echo
So blinding
And you, been quite cold
In your January heat
Wearing the sweater I made
From bailing twine and lizard skin

Shouldn't hate so much
It would take the edge off
The psychological isolation
Under your feet

Paint yourself with burnt amber
And dance with the fire
To forget who you are once again

CREATION

You are nothing but a concoction
of wet dreams and spit.

In a world of angry tears and black holes
you leave nothing to be desired.

You're a thief of fragile hearts
and feed on broken dreams.

An emotional vampire searching
for your late night feast.
You suck every last drop of life
from those who are weak.

Fair ladies being pulled on leashes
like dogs and soiled by deceit,
you are not my master.

You are nothing but lifeless bones,
you are nothing but a nightmare
of your own harsh intentions.

You give off the illusion that you
stand tall but eventually things fade.

When the time comes no one will be there
to catch you when you fall.

THE SADDEST SONG

The great sea can swallow anything,
natives have lost their music notes
just standing on its edge.
Even a blink of an eye may catch
a speck of its nothingness.

Flashes of luminosity burns the eyes
of wandering travelers.
Their blindness leads them
through endless trails of
unwritten songs.

Innocent breaths have been swallowed
inside the vacant darkness.
You hear them whispering
among the mountain tops
when the sun goes silent.

Dark rivers flow with such rage,
dreams die here before they are born.
Shadows laugh at strangers
as they stumble in the dark
to capture their hearts.

Falling hard on their knees,
scraping their skin to bleed.
They pray to anyone who will hear,
pray to anyone who will listen,
pray to anyone willing to save them.

Time is slipping off the edge.
The hands of the clock spiral down
to the depths of the unknown.
Voices echo through the break

of a symphony.
The music stops,
violins crash,
lovers stop the dance.
The spotlight dims
to end the masquerade.

This is the chance to be awakened.
This is the chance to find the light.
This is the time to ask for forgiveness.
This is the time to come back to life.

GHETTO SUNSHINE

Duct tape can fix
a broken heart for only
a little while.

You will then need a
shot of tequila,
a loaded pistol,
and a pair of
comfortable shoes.

That's because
all women know
you can't run fast in
a pair of stilettos
without scuffing
the heels.

DREAM WAKING

Sleepless eyes walk into sirens
that buzz in the lumberjack yard.
Screams come out among
                Artichoke trees
that gag between bullet hole wounds.

Am I dreaming?
Conceal tied tongue lies
and surrender my soul.

NEXT IN LINE

Your presence resembles a dirty martini,
she only drinks it when she's thirsty.
You know you're pretty useless otherwise.

One day you called her a whore
as if it were a dirty word,
she took it as a compliment.

She doesn't need you and you're scared.
You're secretly in love but
you know your time is running thin.

She gets what she asks for.
A buffet table with too many choices,
she's always hungry.

There's a bowl full of candy
and she's tasting every possible flavor,
her favorite is coconut and cream.

You will wait
and wait.

She licks her empty glass clean
and enjoys every last drop.
She'll leave with a smile on her face.

You hear her nails digging
in his back and picture the spring
in her step when she walks out.

Your heart breaks every time
she says she will be late.

You know she's having
a good time without you
and it's eating you up inside.

You can't be the first
but you can be next.
Take a number and get in line,
she's not coming home tonight.

CITY LIGHTS

Passion had hungry eyes to set sail
But lost sight of her destination
Went to Vegas instead
Became a showgirl dressed in red
And she danced
       and she danced

Eyes of indigo and hair of honey
Below the spotlight
Baby is now a star
She would dance
       she would dance

Passion one day
Dropped to the sky where flowers die
And no longer could
dance
dance

Spirit became her crack pipe
In a heroin spoon. Mama
Would have been proud to know
Her little girl is a high rolling whore
And she could fly
       and she could fly

Passion lost sight of her destination
An abandoned soul with a heart of glass
Her vanity faded and no longer could
dance
dance

UNPRETTY

I don't know who I am any more.
I look in the mirror and sense I'm lost.
There's a stranger looking back at me
wondering, "Who is this foreign face?"
Something is different.

Every part of my being detaches away
faster than anything I have witnessed.
Without a warning, the harshness of a void
seeps into my bones unnoticed.

My head spins out of control,
clustered thoughts clog my brain
and I just can't think clearly.
What the hell is happening to me?

This new life in my stomach is to blame.
This uninvited creature is taking my everything.
It's all blank, an unwritten chapter.
Everything is erased before thoughts are clear.

No one prepares you for such a downfall.
How can something so small have this
much power over my entire universe?

Everything seems to change shape
right in front of my eyes.
I become some sort of monster,
I am now some freak show.

The cavity of my stomach is growing.
My eyes tired, breasts enlarged and tender.
My belly swollen to the point where I cannot
see my own cunt.

Do you see a glowing smile on this face?
Pacing the floor, I'm disillusioned.
This changes everything I stood for,
who I am is no more.

This new life is consuming everything I once knew.
It gets harder to breath, harder to swallow.
The night has been reborn to unpretty.

I KNEW A MAN ONCE

I knew a man
once

who thought he could
spit fire

I am fire
and he was not a man.

BUT YOUR OWN

Fueled up
but got nowhere to go.
Driving at sundown
with a broken radio.

Looking at the reflection
in the rearview,
are objects really closer
then they appear?

Fine lines seem to jump out
and say, "We are here."
Black circles smother eyes,
too many sleepless nights.

Streets begin to blend together.
Doesn't matter the route you take,
you end up in a far off place.

Each window to the outside
carries the same old story,
someone's living or dying.

Highways grasp what can't been seen,
too fast can it be taken away.
No directions come with the package,
figures.

This is life
driving endlessly with no purpose
but your own.

WORDS

I wonder sometimes
what people think of
me after they read
one of my psychotic creations.

I imagine they are thinking,
Lock her up and throw
away the key!

Don't think
I haven't heard the stories.
I must admit,
my writing has
more life to it than you or I.

My words have lived, died,
even committed suicide.
They loved,
they fucked
with your mind.

Some say I'm pure genius
but it's not me that needs
the recognition, much
rather the lives other than
mine give inspiration.

Words can express anything.
Live on the pages
and mingle with your thoughts,
deep thoughts.

Mixed emotions slip up
and you begin to

lose yourself deeply.

The exterior hides many
great things,
unseen things.

It is amazing what just
a few words can do
to affect one's mind.

Words are powerful,
very powerful.
Words are my weapon.

After reading mine
I will have you convinced
that you are the one who is
completely insane.

YOU SAVED ME

for Lenin

You saved me
from starless nights
and endless traffic jams.

I would sit and gaze out
my window what seemed like hours
wondering if there is a purpose to
breathing in the darkest of days.

I'd listen to the song of birds.
I'd watch the match being
lit for a cigarette.

Searching clues that come
with this scavenger hunt
but nothing came to mind.

I would write line after line
and page after page until
my knuckles bled.

Tossing and turning while
the moon was high,
the air thick like winter.
Thinking, waiting, still nothing.

Since you have been in my life
there are no more days of
something missing,
no more nights of dreamless sleep.

You have awakened the child in my bones.

You have awakened something new.
Saving the last bit of innocence
that has yet been lost.

How I remember now what
it's like to see the world
with curious eyes and wondering hands.

STARVING ARTIST

I have been missing
for quite some time.
Hiding between colorless clouds
overlooking the deepest ocean.
My lips have become mute
against the yellow sand.

I walk here in the quiet of thoughts
feeling hungry for something real.
Phantoms are sighing
each time a page is turned.
Each time a verb or noun is forgotten
a breath is taken away.

I can't make the past disappear,
I bear my scars as a reminder of hope.
I'm going to bite the bullet
and let it take me to glowing street lamps.
I'm convinced new channels
will find their way to my pen.

As moments flash, a day passes.
Time doesn't wait for tomorrow.
The beauty of falling down is
picking yourself up and letting go.
It's easy to be swallowed whole,
the hard part is being reborn.

RAW

for my muse

I remember the first time

You opened the door
And I instantly got sucked
Into your eyes like tiny vacuums

You look like the hot flesh of sun
Smell of sex and Park Avenue

You don't say a word, just smiled
Put a finger to my lips
SShhh...

You have me right where you want me
On your bed sideways pointing west

You whisper in my ear
All the dirty things you're gonna do

You're a machine made of chrome
You tug my hair and call me baby

Fuck me nine ways to Sunday
Grip my flesh as if your life depends on it
Leave your mark with your teeth

Feel me from the inside out
Tear me up and taste my mouth

Take me on a bullet trip
Pistol whip

For this night you own me, all of me
Take me any way you need
Any way you want

Nail me hardcore
Drive me down like a terrorist
In the midsummer heat

Can't get enough of your violating hands
You're my addiction, I want more

I will never recover
From your drug induced
sex bomb

IF ONLY

for the lone soldier

I'm mourning the time we never had,
the words that never escaped my lips.

Moments have come and gone.
I write poems to feel closer to you.

All this time I've tried to forget you
but I lose myself between heartbreak
and Lovers Avenue.

There are hours of written
love letters you will never read.
They remain untouched in a suitcase
marked, "If Only".

I'll keep writing in the hopes
of maybe someday.

SOMEWHERE HERE

Through
the looking glass
got dirt in my eye

Scratched the surface
but I'm fine

Running and running
but not enough
faster
       than an eagle flies

Sweat beads down
the periscope blinds
as reality fades

And I swear to you
I will find salvation
somewhere here
tonight

FOR THE BLOOMING POET

The first poem
you will ever write
will be the doorway
to many endeavors.

It will be revolutionary,
write what you feel
without holding back.

Let emotions run wild
on the page, you can build
something extraordinary
if you don't try so hard.

Let random thoughts
rain on your parade.
Offer them a drink,
a stiff one
to loosen up the progress.

You may find it easier
to chase the vowels.

DO NOT BE AFRAID

At birth, our death

is already marked.

Each day that passes,

we are closer to dying.

Life can break into

different pieces

and brings us

to different places

as time rolls on.

Do not be afraid

of what life could bring.

We all feel the hurt,

we all feel the joy.

The more we feel,

the more human we become.

Hop on the saddle

and ride into the darkness,

leave your fear behind.

Tip your hat to the shadows

and become one with

the taste of panic.

Blow up the silence

and let your voice be heard.

Show no mercy,

it's you against life,

take it for a ride.

THE HUNTER

I like to play with fire
and sleep for days

I sharpen my teeth
before leaving the house
in case I get hungry

After each feast I lick my
fingers clean

You can find me howling
at the moon during
the dead hours

I sleep with my eyes open
I own the night

I am a hunter of prism dreams
and endless memories

Swallowing them whole
like a snake, digesting them
nice and slow to feel them squirm

WHAT GOES AROUND COMES AROUND

I never took a writing class.
Maybe that's obvious
but I don't need structure.

I've been known to do things
my way anyways.
If you think my writing sucks
you don't have to read it.

At least I have the courage
to share my life with others
in the hopes that it will amuse
some poor sap out there.

Even after all the mistakes I've made,
all the headaches, all the
"I fucked up" moments,
I believe my life is worth something.

Call me shallow but I don't see you
accomplishing anything other than
running around in circles with
your tail between your legs.

I mean, you are exactly in
the same place where you left me
and that was ages ago.
Karma is a bitch ain't it?

LOVE AFFAIR

For just a moment

I want to feel your grasp

We could run away

For just a moment

Without judging eyes

To a secret place

For just a moment

Where we could leave

Our footprints to live

The way we couldn't

For just a moment

THIS ONE'S FOR YOU KID

for A. B.

She doesn't leave the house
without hand sanitizer.
Carries a can of pepper spray
to ward off strangers.

Her name is I'll kick you
in your two front teeth if
you look at me for too long.

She doesn't have patience
for bad drivers.
She's lovely and can be sweet.

Blames her crazy alcoholic mother
for her own crazy ass.
Went from blonde to brown
to darken the mood.

These days the bedroom doesn't
get dressed up for company.
Nights are filled with
lost love and masturbation.

Used and abused, beaten down
by her own rough edges.
The type of girl who
looks in the mirror too loosely.

Been burned too many times,
yet finds the strength to
show off the ashes.

31

Foreplay is a must,
loves sex but hates chatter.
She wears red well.

Goes after what she can't have
so she won't get knocked down
as hard.

When nobody is looking,
she'll smother a feather
in bathwater trying
to absorb its lightness.

Doesn't take sugar in her tea,
might make her pucker up
in all the wrong places.

Weekends come and go,
night clubs aren't her scene.
She has a romance with
a cocktail and sushi.

She says she doesn't care too much.
I know deep down she uses
her skin as a coat of armor.

If you knew her like I do,
you would understand
why she doesn't leave fingerprints
on the wall before leaving a room.

POETRY SLAM

This ain't no poem
about butterflies or candy canes.
Listen up fools!
Why are you here?

The lone poets,
all sitting here waiting to
share their words written out
in blood from cluster fuck dreams.

No one will remember your shit.
Your nouns and verbs
won't go beyond these cement walls.

Want your voice to be heard?
Walk out the door right now
and climb to the highest mountain.
Say it loud!

Call out to the children
who want to learn about
shattered heartbreaks
and run-on sentences.

Call out to the ones
who will not only hear you
but will listen.

Make them listen!
Point your finger in their faces,
talk with your hands.

Get your point across
with any means necessary.

Take their ears hostage,
run their hearts in the ground.

Don't let them shut their eyes,
don't let them ignore the truth.
Make your voice be carried
near and far.

Throw around your madness,
make them ask about your native tongue,
show them where you came from.

This ain't no poem
about butterflies or candy canes.
This ladies and gentleman
is a poem about making a difference.

EMBRACE THE STORM

All the trees are turning gray
in your forest, she must be dying.
Oceans have hushed against the sand
and the sun doesn't speak
as high as it used to,
what has changed you?

It seems the rain occupies this space
more and more each day.
You remain cradled in the ruins
as if you don't notice
what's happening on the outside.

Everything is fading so fast.
Dull music slips through the cracks
and nothing is what it used to be.
I ran into the nucleus
of your thoughts, it's wandering.

I saw pieces of your past
flashing through your eyes.
I felt as if I was watching a
silent film running in slow motion.

Thunder rumbles in the distance
with a threatening voice, it's waiting.
Lightening flickers with the urge
to take you hostage.

It spiders down almost touching you,
then springs back with an echoed silence that
could break glass with teeth.

My life was yours for the taking.

I offered my blood, sweat, and tears
but instead you pushed yourself
deeper in the silent cavern
of your solitary confinement.

I wanted to be the one who
could silence your pain
but you were living on borrowed time.

CRAZED PARADE

I want you to tell me
what it is that you seek
Hiding secrets between your teeth

The rabid star hanging from
your arm hasn't been afraid
Kiss my sleek aquamarine

Spin the monkey into a coffin
and spit in the grave
Dance atop the tombstone
this could be home sweet home

Forbid the rambling puppets
they are not wise
If quiet you hear the answers
wallowing between crooked tongues

This night is a virgin
praise the twilight serpent
Violet pillows whisper upon
such porcelain skin

What name do you give
your great mother?
She's dirty from back seats
and abandoned alleys

She cries quite a mystic river
Angels laugh uncontrollably as
she burns in sinful delight

Drinking holy water to
understand faith but it has no taste

A prisoner can't
bite the freedom on this train
A day goes by and we still
come out empty handed

Insomnia comes to teach
lessons from the old crow
but the pages were empty

Stars of glass fall out of place
but hunger did not find its way
as I stumble to find the right pace

The Jack-in-the-box is dancing
in your silver sequined cocktail dress
How dare he without permission

His painted mask has been
scraped with razorblades again
He shouldn't play with such sharp
objects without a straightjacket on

Oh hale Mary, kiss the royal thumb
and tell us a bed time story
about paper airplanes and chrome
cities

Let's fly to the end of the world
Tonight is mine and yours
May the moon hang low and bright

There is nothing left here
but poker faces and joker smiles
Nuns run wild here like crazed animals

Let's not forget our umbrella
in case it rains

Black holes rule here

Fly away, fly away with me
to the next freak show
made of purple skies
and gasoline oceans

UNFAITHFUL

Yes she was unfaithful to you,
guilty as charged

She told me she would visualize
you being someone else because
of your dullness between the sheets

She said you told her you never
got complaints

Believe me,
she sure wasn't lying

THIS POEM

This poem, keep it close
It will teach you things
Love it unconditionally
And it will love you back

A collage of words that nobody
Can take away from you
Your trusty companion

All yours

Forever

Tuck it under your pillow at night
For safe keeping
It may save you one day when you
Are at a loss for words
Or when you need a little shove

DEEP

I want in
under your bed

Abandon me
among the debris
that lies

I want to belong
with the earth
and meat of
its existence

Feel me
feel the weakness

Secrets hibernate here
Slumber with me
please

with me

I will beg passing cars

IT'S BEEN SO LONG

I loved the feel of
your razor to my blade
I ached for your
tongue to choke my mouth

I couldn't get enough
of your disease
Your voice was sharp
and your touch was raw

You were a wild fire
and I can't tell you
how much I loved
to get burned

I loved drowning
in your poison
I loved being shackled
to your mind

I breathed in your toxins
I drank your venom
like water

I liked the way you tied
my hands in barbwire
I loved the way your knife
felt scraping against my skin

I'd roll around in your sickness
I would rub myself down
with your biohazard waste

I miss tracing my fingertips

through your gunpowder
I miss dodging your grenades

I would suck on the rusty nails
you left behind every time
you went away

I ache for you to come back soon
because it's been so long since
you have torched my atom bomb

"You are the only woman I know that
can turn any gay man straight."
-Juan

WEAKNESS

I built a house today out of
newspaper and matches

It was very affectionate

But when I lit it on fire
it became alive
and stole my bones

WRITINGS ON THE WALL

*You never know what you're gonna find written on the
bathroom wall*

Jen and Katie were here on 10/10/03
Joey fucked my brains out
Liz rocks

Melissa loves Matt
Megan and Amanda will be friends forever
We are the shit!

He ain't worth it, choke him dead!
If only she had a gun
I will rule the world

Dillon wore my undies
Jimmy's dick is huge!
Alex is a douchebag

I'll run you under the bus bitch!
Die! Die! Die!

Tracy is a lesbo
For a good time call Jessie Mills
I am Miss Thang

Kristen likes pussy
I'm sooooo drunk!
Josh is a baby
Fuck you morons!

Love my friends cuz
we are fuckin hot!
Young + Pretty

Men are assholes
OMGWTFBBQ
Love you more bitch!
I sucked Kevin's dick last night

Tara will get her ass kicked
James got fucked last night
Beth has Aids
Lena is a rabid animal

You only live once
but memories never die
Best time of my life!

Need a whore?
Call 1-800-ANGRY-VAGINA
*Caution: may cause herpes

I saw the silver lining
hidden in the mushroom cloud

Music = Life
We will all be saved because
the hamster is watching you.

BIRTH

for all my babies

I have been knocked up so many times
I can't tell you how many babies I've given birth to
It's the only kind of pain worth going through

All the love poems, all the hate poems
All the hours wasting away in the darkness alone

Composing life, composing death

They are worth the time digging
Through the memories you wish
You didn't remember

They are worth the torment from
The new wounds that surface

They are worth every ounce of sacrifice
Because they are the only ones who won't
Turn on you

I DON'T WANT TO REMEMBER

I don't want to remember
the rain without you

The laughs with tears in our eyes

Being wrapped in your splendor
on cold nights

I don't want to remember
watching you while you slept

Holding your hand

The way your skin felt

I don't want to remember
the way you smelled

The curve of your lips

The taste of your mouth

I don't want to remember how much
I miss you

Because it hurts too much to believe
we had to say good bye

BED OF NIGHT

Father I have sinned,
touched the sweet flower
with rabid thorns once again.

There is no one else to blame,
I'll spend the night in a death box.

Fuck the angels I say, where are they
when you need them most?

I fly through the night feeling
sand in my eyes.
Paper cuts can't heal,
I am falling to the trees.

I begin to feel weak,
my bones are shaking.
I taste the rain in my mouth
when I breath in.

The ocean sweeps me
under its blanket
while the horizon
seduces the night.

My heart is flooding,
my veins are tangled up,
my time is running out.

I grasp all the things
that no one else can touch
to keep them safe.

Here is my resting place,

next to yours.

Tell me, can you hear
my whispers in your sleep?

FALL OF LIFE

Leaves escape the comfort
of the stem

like you

Harboring in the autumn sun

These waking moments
fade over time

like you

The wind, hissing in the distance
burns my ears fire red

What is this secret

like you

SHE TOLD ME ONCE

A man is a martyr
if he lives outside you

FOR THE BOY WHO DOESN'T SLEEP

I'm now just a figment of your imagination
A dead girl kept on ice
The one you leave on the back burner
"Just in case"

You don't get rid of my number
because you will need it later for drunk dialing
You will tell me how much you love me
and how much it hurts that I'm not there

I should stop over so we can talk
You will even make coffee
I will have to remind you it's 4am
and I have moved on
That I'm sleeping next to him right now

You tell me about the girl you hooked up with
because she didn't mind your bad habits
You'll tell me how sorry you are
You beg me to come back
You tell me it will be different this time

None of it matters now
You should have thought of me
before you fucked her
Or maybe you did but didn't think
you were in the wrong because
your dick was doing all the talking

I know you didn't call to talk
I know you don't give a damn that I drink it black
I know you're looking for just the sex
Because it's been a while and you're lonely
and you're drunk and you're lonely

I'm the dead girl kept on ice just in case
you're having one of those nights
when you need somebody
to pick up the phone

AFTER MIDNIGHT

Eyelids shut after
a long day of yearning
of telling a story
about oneself

Here all is silent
except for the humming
of the mind at work

This is the time
to ask for things
that you were too afraid
to utter past your lips

Those things that are
most sacred
most seductive

Those things would be
things of the marvelous
the things that dreams
become inside you

IT WAS THE WAY

It was the way
you looked at me
that made me
melt between
car seats

I study your profile
to find some trace
of my belonging
here

A song plays
on the radio
and you look
at me as if it
meant something

You smile for
a moment
and turn away
as we continue
to fake our
happiness

WHAT IS LOVE ANYWAY?

I know the perfect man is out there and I won't stop having meaningless sex until I find him - A. M. Black

Hit up the town
Paint it black
With princess heels
And long nails

Cranberry and cream
Vodka bean
Set the stage
Dance to be

Malibu machine
Kick the tune
On a new trip
How fabulous

Tattoo her request
On your chest
Label it loud
And deep

Sinister bitch
The glass is
Almost empty
Black tie junkie

Fill it up gently
Haul ass home
What the fuck is
Love anyway?

Bang to please

Shot of ecstasy
Wiped a tongue
On a sleeve

Feel her scream
Pause the frame
Bite the need
Touch the seed

Baby please
Worship the queen
As she starts
A fresh new scene

IT WASN'T THERE TO BEGIN WITH

They ask me why I don't
write something a little
less dismal this time
but I don't have it in me.

Isn't there enough bullshit poems
written out there about being in love
and happily ever after?

Most of the time it doesn't work out
because the "happy" never existed
in the first place.

It was only a one night stand
that became a false pretense to a trap
most of you call a relationship.
Wake up and smell the coffee people.

MEMORY

We are silent haters
communicating through
memories and tears

We are silent lovers
communicating through
poetry and lyrics

KISS

A kiss

more intimate than

Your floating
warm

You feel sensual
and alluring

A kiss

more intimate than

You feel unstoppable
touching

Just one kiss
one needs to be fulfilled

THE BREAKUP

When you finally leave his ass
you'll change your lipstick color
and stay up past midnight
with your high heels still on

You will cut out his picture
and insert an underwear model
At last you are the keeper of
all the remote controls

Throw away those little keepsakes
like that bubble gum machine ring
and a teddy bear that wears a t-shirt
that reads "Happy Valentine's Day"

You enjoy waking up next to an empty space
because your feet have more room
It will be liberating

You can't remember the last time
you had this much freedom
You breath in the fresh air and smile
This is the first day of the rest of your life

EVEN HEROS SLIP AWAY

Love hurts,
rejection finding its way
down your throat
stinging thoughts of happier times.

The liquor store is expecting you,
its arms reaching out to embrace
what's left of your humanity.

They say you can find dead poets here.
Many suicide notes have been composed
in this very parking lot.
Written and rewritten to get the words just right.

You can almost hear the funeral music
playing loosely in the balmy summer morning.
Looking at your watch, it's only 10:00 am.

Love hurts
and here you are again.
Attempting to wash away your emotions
with silent promises from a bottle.

Sometimes even heroes slip away
but every second counts
to make up for lost time.

AFTERLIFE

Taking others
by the hand to the stars

Reaching towards
changing lifetimes and laughing

FEVER

Look at me
I'm flying high
In a cobra sky

Stars like diamonds
Crashing together
What a pretty picture

It's a lovely night
To watch it all burn down
From here

It's time to slip away
Because life is already
Dead in my head

Catch me drifting
In the folds of the wind
Like a weightless airplane

Here you will find that
Love will attack you blind
Sweet suicide

Don't leave me behind
Angels tonight
I might see mine

IT'S MY TIME

You could say I have
been through a lot of shit
back in the days between
monkey bars and after parties.
Times have changed and seasons have passed.

I have braved through heartbreak,
running on empty, and bad weather.
Everyone told me I wouldn't make it
as a writer.

It's years later and I'm here,
author of my life, an artist of words.

A mother
a fighter
a lover
a go getter
So far things have worked
in my favor.

All those who have judged me in the past
are two, three, even four steps behind me.

I'm not glamorous
but I'm not that plain.
I'm not famous
but I'm not that ordinary.

I'm not sure how far
I've traveled but I have
walked among a thousand stars.

I've met quite a few sharp shooters

riding high horses back in the day
wearing plastic smiles and expensive perfume.
They all had something in common,
they weren't sure what direction they
were headed.

I'm moving forward with my head held high,
travel the road they said no one could survive.

I live for those moments,
It's going be one hell of a ride
and I can't wait to embrace it.

Maybe someday you assholes
will find your way.

HOLLOW NIGHT

This hollow night
is composed of
crippled dreams
longing to be with you

again

I twist myself up
in the sheets like a
straitjacket
while the cold air
nuzzles my face

becoming frosty

It's these times
I wish to be
someone else

But there is no
someone else
No one should
have to feel this
alone

COLD LIKE WINTER

I can't bear to see you dying,
I'm fragile like a house made of glass.
Tell me you will stay with me always
even if it means nothing now.

I see it in your eyes as
frostbite filters on cracked stone.
My lips are frozen shut, it's getting cold.
Please don't leave me this way.

I will be alone with nothing
but sympathy cards and blood flowers.

I'll be engulfed with insomnia,
waiting for you to knock on the window
and steal me away.

I see it in your skin, it's time to go.
I hold your hand,
you tell me I'll be just fine.

Watching you slip away in the getaway car,
my body is shutting down,
I think my heart just stopped.

I can't breathe, I can't move.
I become a lifeless arrow.
How do you speak of the dead?

I'm going to evaporate,
stick to the walls like vapor
and hope to be licked clean.

IF DREAMS MAY NEVER COME

I am dead among wolves.
The silence is so heavy
even echoes can't be heard.

Something is changing.
In these times eyes look in dark corners.
This is where shadows are kings
and cobwebs thread the history
of what has been.

Battlefields of dead carcasses
haunt what cannot be forgotten.
These ghosts are very unforgiving.

Lives have lived and lives have died.
The past can't disappear,
truth and lies go hand in hand.

One can't exist without the other.
So what is there to believe in
if dreams may never come?

PROFESSIONAL KILLER

I can over run your playground
by just a glance
Torch your body in an instant
with a wicked grin

Make you sit in a corner
with a gun to your head
I'd like to see you splattered
on the walls over and over again

Talk dirty to me baby
tell me you're dying
tell me you feel pain
whisper in my ear
that death is a beautiful thing

I will bite my nails in anticipation
just the thought of you fading
gets me off

I am your god
a venomous kiss
a pretty blood flower
don't fuck with me cause
I am your killer

My beautiful sunshine
I'll pull the drapes over your eyes
With a simple click of my heels
I can make your nightmares come alive

Snapping my fingers
you drop to your knees
Bow to me

bow to me baby

Oh I am a breath taking hazard
I almost can't take how scandalous I am

I look in the mirror and ask myself
how can I be so sinfully charming
But it is you who has made me
this way my dearest love

BENEATH

Reality can be unfolded

If discovered

What is sensual

Alluring

Unique

Is behind the possibility

The novelty

Ripened

Adventure

Is waiting

Remove the mask

Look into the world

With virgin eyes

THE WAKING EYE

It is that time
our illusion of happiness is vanishing

We live dreams
of wanting, of breathing, of loving
the one who cups our heart passionately

It is all ignored and hushed
We sweep life under a blanket
while war begins with the serpent

Buttered hands make the attempt
to bring back the hours before
the softness fades

All goes quiet when the horizon falls
What if this is all that's left?

What if we have become
so calloused with our cruel ways?

We bleed like an abstract painting
hungry for the truth but we are denied

Tumbling through a fortress
while breathing in the air as thick as tar
We are not one with our sanctuary

The sun filters its rays with such grace
Rivers run with no shame but we live like thieves

Guilt escapes to dance on rooftops
like no tomorrow
We are the ones who become fools

Mother earth calls out to the ones
who wear chastity belts
to attempt to clean up the mess
that settled after the storm

Death walks here with open eyes
To give is to receive and to receive is to die
with emptiness out on the open range

IF I WAS A PAINTING

If I was a painting
I'd be abstract with
blues and grays

A hidden message
would be written
in between each
fold of color
for only your eyes
to understand

But you seem to
always miss the
beginning

I HOLD HANDS

I hold hands

with a burden.

Trying to shake it loose

but the grip only

becomes stronger.

I feel an electric circuit

through my veins,

I'm growing tired from fighting

the same war over and over.

Like a skipping record,

I can only remember

the part that repeats.

It starts to burn a hole

in my eyesight and

I start to lack stable

moments of thinking,

Someone please shut off the lights!

Nothing is left

but a cave made of

broken love letters

and a stale appetite.

I try to decipher

if my life lives

through my words

or if my words

become my life.

LADY ON A WIRE

I'll burn my clothes
Scrub my skin in the shower
till it's raw

Cover my tracks
with empathy and surprise
when I see the crime scene

I'll run away for a while
Use a different name
Cut off all ties to people
I once knew

I'll make new friends
in high places to bail me out
if I get caught on my knees

I'll bury the gun in my mouth
and smile wide
Everyone around me won't
suspect a damn thing

I'll throw myself against
the world without any hesitation
I'm trigger happy
and you can't hold it against me

You should save yourself
while you can still taste me
Beauty kills baby
beauty kills

"Revenge looks good on you."
-C. Bedford

FEATHER BED

We have become daydreamers
of things not yet written
and night dreamers of things
long gone past

Everything in between is yours
to trace

When the time comes
a soft voice will lure us to sleep
in the hopes of everything
becoming erased

LOVE POEM TO A STRANGER

I don't know you
but I want to kiss your lips

I want to feel your skin
against my naked palms

Let's become wrapped
in wonder while dreaming

I don't know you
but you are the essence
that floods my autumn sun

Puzzle pieces we are that fit
together so perfectly

So lovely
we become the whispers
in each other's breath

THE BIG BANG

You're nothing but a
schizophrenic love song
with a knife to your throat.

When you speak, your lips
fumble for the right syllables.

You wear a fabricated steel coat
and bruised skin.
You eat a big bowl
of "I don't give a fuck"
for breakfast.

Secretly you cry yourself
to sleep every night
while tucked in the safety
of your sheets.

Your eyes are made of mirrors.
Reflecting what they see
so no one can touch you.

A girl should know
that a loaded gun is
incapable of falling in love.

NOCTURNALLY YOURS

Wandering loosely
I forget what day it is
I forget what street I'm traveling
I don't even know who I am any more

The air is thick with infection and
I have a stale taste in my mouth
It's like one big carnival
and the rides aren't free

You never know who could be watching
without you realizing it
I find your hiding place
by trespassing that sacred space

Dead men shouldn't be able to
make you cry
but they find ways to disrupt
the garden with stone roses

Black flies infest the forest
blinding heroes on white horses
Love is a martyr
standing close to watch
everything fall apart

The wind nips my earlobes
begging me to scream
but no sound comes out
It all becomes more complicated

The twilight has come home from her travels
I look to where you use to sleep
there's nothing but blood stained sheets

Nothing surrounds me except
the voices I hear at night
isolating me from touching new pavement

I have to be reminded
you can't kill the dead with echoes
Weeds are caught in my throat
I'm suffocating

This is all the same illusion
I witnessed in the mirror before
I slumbered in the shadows
so I wouldn't be seen by thieves

Only I am guilty of caring too much
only I am guilty of holding back tears
only I am punished from the pain I suffered

Without a light I cannot see
through the doorway of freedom
Having the power to ignite its flame
I hold an unlit torch

I am held back with the memories
I don't want to let go
I torture myself in this fashion
day after day
night after night
I have become nocturnally yours

I LOOK BACK

I look back
and remember
how you fought
to keep your blood
and how you fought
to lose mine

It's been a few months
of unspoken words
and I watch from afar
as you try to soak up
the stains from the pavement

LOVE IS A DRUG

Crash

Boom

Hiss

This is your brain on love

Crash

Boom

Hiss

This is your brain on high

Crash

Boom

Hiss

This is your brain when it dies

Crash

Boom

Hiss

This is your brain when it doesn't heal

Crash

Boom

Hiss

Any questions?

JUST FOR STARTERS

for the gentlemen who aren't gentlemen

I'm tired of all those idiots
who think they can have any girl
by merely saying hello
while giving that wise-ass look
because they think they are all that.
Who the hell do they think they are?

Slapping around their dick like
an untamed beast,
is that supposed to be impressive?
PLEASE!
I'm more of an untamed beast
than any penis can claim.

I'm untouchable
and gorgeous
and there is nothing
any of you can do about it.

First things first, put that
one-eyed jackhammer back in your pants
then simply shower us ladies with
something we like to call
R E S P E C T!

Then you can get up early to
make breakfast and fetch
the morning paper.
Whisper sweet nothings in our ear
from time to time just to see us smile.

Take the dog for a long walk

around the block in a blizzard
so we don't catch a cold.
Get on all fours. You heard me right,
to scrub the floor.
We want to be able see our reflection
while we walk high and proud.

Send us flowers while
we are busting our asses at work
trying to make ends meet.
Show off those not so good
writing skills to compose
a goofy love poem
and slip it in our lunch bag.

Be a real man and do the laundry.
While you're at it clean out
the fridge of all those leftovers
you refused to eat.
Maybe go to the grocery store
without hitting the express line.

Call our mother to invite her to
the fabulous dinner you prepared.
Take her coat when she arrives
and treat her like the queen that
she is.

Light candles and hand us
a glass of wine to relax while
in the bath that you drew.
Massage our tired skin and kiss us softly
until we fall asleep.

That's just for starters. I could go on,
but I hope you get the idea.
Have mercy on your soul if you don't.

There's more to me, the tall blonde,
or the sassy brunette you men keep eyeing.
There's more than tits and ass.

That MORE is
passion, strength, dreams, and desire.

Us ladies have the power, the urge.
We have what it takes to be a
one woman machine.
Nice guys always finish last,
so keep that dick in your pants.

TINY DANCER

for Halo

As I look in your eyes
I see a little piece
of myself looking back.
My reflection smiles
and whispers my name.

I'm drawn to this unconditional love,
the freshness of innocence.
Grasp it tightly because
life will chip away at it
as days run short
and nights run long.

Travel light,
there will be times
you wished you had
a little more room.

There's so much to feel,
take the time to soak it in.
Bend the rules,
fly the night,
break hearts,
dance till you can't dance any more.

The world is waiting to meet you.
You're only young once
so jump in with both feet
and swim like hell.

CONFESSIONS

I make an entrance
I live in moments
I work only part of the time
I talk a lot when I like you
I wish I could fly
I enjoy time spent alone
I look at each day as a new beginning
I bend the rules
I find I am everything and everything in between
I listen to the voices you cannot hear
I hide what I really think
I pray I will get caught in the rain, again
I walk with attitude
I write to be inspired
I see the things that make you blind
I sing in the shower then lie about it
I laugh even if it isn't funny
I can do most anything
I always win in the end
I let my imaginations run wild
I get anything my heart desires
I put on a happy face even when I'm not
I watch to learn
I want to be what you thought I could not
I will become what you thought I could not
I cry just to feel the tears
I make mistakes and do them again
I love to feel
I hate closed mindedness
I sometimes think the world should start over
I touch minds with fucked up words of wisdom
I hurt you when you're not around
I think outside of the box
I kissed a girl

I did it more than once
I read your eyes before you say a word
I fear I won't age gracefully
I hope I will
I break things trying to put them together
I quit being on time
I drink the sun and breath the moon
I hug my ambitions
I miss being someone new
I forgive but don't forget
I drive a not so fancy car
I have enemies due to jealousy
I miss old friends
I say things I don't mean
I dance when no one is looking
I try different directions
I don't let most people get too close
I believe we are not the only ones
I feel unbreakable
I know your dirty little secrets
I wonder if I'm the only one with answers
I only have a little while
I may tell you otherwise
I dream big
I go out with a bang

PRETTY LITTLE THOUGHTS

I ain't your normal sunshine. I greet the day with a warning label, I fucking hate this town. I hate so much I could stop an oncoming train. It's dangerous to be kind because they'll shit on you no matter what. They think they're above the world. I should do something about it, but I feel nothing. Nothing.

They just want to control what's not theirs. Don't look at me in that tone of voice. I can suck up all the stars in your night and spit them out like worthless seeds. I bleed for miles, I have bled for miles. I feel nothing. Nothing.

They won't appreciate you. They take everything in and throw it out. They weep, they beg. Their obnoxious stares burn holes in my head. I will kill, kill them dead. I will leave clues as to where I leave them. I will draw a map, but I feel nothing. Nothing.

LIFE AS WE KNOW IT

Life as we know it ends badly. There are only three things we talk about when we hit the ages of liver spots and hip replacements. These are construction, the weather, aches and pains. That ladies and gentleman marks our death.

When all you got to say is "My hip was giving me some trouble while it was raining near that damn intersection that was blocked off," save everyone else the hassle and pack your own shit. You can forget your beach hat and sunglasses, it ain't sunny where you're going. The only place you're headed is six feet down.

POETRY IS A MISTRESS

When I'm in my element
I suffer from insomnia
Words will hit me like a car crash
In the burning months

Verses form without any
Thought process
My hand glides back and forth
Back and forth
Faster and faster
Along the pages

The friction becomes so intense
The paint on the walls peel
That's when you know
The night is on its way
To writing the greatest poem
Ever written

Poetry, you are one hell of a mistress
We belong together
I will share this poem with the world
And then lie through my teeth
When they ask if it's about you
It will be our dirty little secret

YOU AND I

I walked along
a storefront window
and could have swore
I saw a reflection of
your ghost standing next to me.

It's funny how much
you have taken over my thoughts.
Maybe they're not my words
I write, but yours.

It would explain a lot of things
like why I wear the dark
as a disguise.

WHEN TIMES ARE HARD

I
When times are hard
you're married to your bed.
The sheets become your icebox,
you swear you're dead.

You found "The One".
The one who was going to replace
all the other fools.

The one you were going to walk
down the aisle with.
In sickness and in health,
till death do us part.

The house with the white picket fence,
host dinner parties,
have his babies.
Sail the world and grow old together.

You were a part of him
and he was a slice of you.
The power couple of envious friends.

The freight train derailed when
you noticed the pink lipstick stain
and the glitter on his shoes.

Said he wants to travel alone.
His way out was fucking a cocktail waitress
who worked at a place called Night Moves.

You throw everything he owns
out on the street in the rain.

You feel somewhat cleansed.
You wish you owned a handgun.

II

I wake up to a phone call at 6 am.
You don't say a word but I hear the sobs.
I already know it's going to be a long day.

I sit with you for comforting.
The television is on but you stare
at the dark smudge on the wall instead.

I watch you sip too much wine
and smoke too many cigarettes.

You're too broken up to dump
the overflowing ashtray,
you move on to a styrofoam cup.
It's like this for hours.

I ask if you want to talk about it
but all you do is let out a drawn out sigh.
Glancing at the ticking clock,
I don't know how much longer I can take.

This isn't going anywhere
and clearly neither are you.
There's only one thing to do
in a crises like this.
Order take out and stock up
on a shit load of Ben and Jerry's.

When times are hard
you're married to your bed.
The sheets become your icebox
and you're dead.

BECOME YOU

We try so hard to stand out,
we become someone else.

Why do we fight to be different?
Where is that going to get you?

What would happen if we stopped
trying to be different and just
became ourselves?

BLANK

I find my secrets
are a great weight
on my shoulders
but I have lacked
a pen to write them.
Putting my lips
to a bottle of gin
in the hopes
of making sense
to random words
but even in quiet places
shadows whisper.

RANDOM THOUGHTS OVER LUNCH

I'm sitting in a dingy diner
with stale, cold food.

I hate stale, cold food
and I hate this shirt I'm wearing.

There's two lesbians opposite me,
one keeps looking at her watch,
the other at me.

I forgot to put my watch on.
Now that I'm thinking about it,
I never wear a watch.

There's a woman walking in.
I can tell by the way she licks her lips
she's a prostitute.

I get pissed off thinking they
get paid big bucks for sex.
I'm not earning big bucks
or getting sex.

A con-artist, now there's a profession
but I'm not a genius.
My sister got the smart genes, bitch.

I do have creativity,
could be a serial killer.

A serial killing rapist of minds
then write a poem about it.

The lesbians are now kissing.

Isn't there a law against
public displays of affection?

I'm not getting any.
Affection sucks.

Back in the college days
you didn't need affection, just a fuck.
Friends with benefits were always
enough.

Now you have to be a lesbian
to get some action? What gives?

Giving. Nobody gives
anything anymore unless
they get something in return.
There's always a motive.

The fan above is rattling.
It will probably fall on my head,
I will have to sue for millions
because I won't be lucky enough
for it to kill me.

The lesbians are now feeling
each other up. I think they forgot
they weren't in the bedroom.

Now I'm just down right irritated,
not because of what I'm witnessing
but because they haven't asked me
to join them.

I'm not greedy. I'm allowed to have
needs. Or are they wants?

I wanted this dress the other day
but it didn't come in my size.
Why are all the large sizes the ones
that are left?

Why do fat girls try to fit into
a pair of leggings? Just because
something is in style doesn't mean
you have a license to wear it.

Like skinny jeans. I'm just not going
to get into it.

I hate shopping, makes me depressed.
When I'm depressed I go shopping.
I don't win either way.

I'm pretty damn angry
because now my coffee is cold
and I haven't seen the waitress
since I got this shitty food.

I think too much,
I'm always thinking.
I guess that's just what writers
do.

HE LOVES ME (NOT)

She tears off
dandelion petals
in desperation for
the answer

He loves me
He loves me not

He loves me
He loves me not

He loves

She always
stops when there's
a few left because
she can't handle the
same damn outcome
every time

ONLY IN HOLLYWOOD

It's only in Hollywood where
you can get away with staring out
from a magazine cover looking like
you haven't ate in days

It's only in Hollywood where
you're not beautiful enough
unless you have something
nipped or tucked

It's only in Hollywood where
a man can beat his wife
to a bloody pulp and get a
slap on the wrist with a book deal

It's only in Hollywood where
somebody is murdered and the
fugitive gets more notoriety

It's only in Hollywood where
you can get away with wearing
too much borrowed bling

It's only in Hollywood where
you can sleep with prostitutes
and be signed on to the next big picture

It's only in Hollywood where
a suicide is blamed because
of too much fame

It's only in Hollywood where
real talent is taken over by
not so "reality" stars

It's only in Hollywood where
bad press can save your career

It's only in Hollywood where
doctors will shoot you up with
too many drugs

It's only in Hollywood where
after you're dead, you will finally
get the recognition you deserve

114

LET'S PRETEND

Let's pretend for this moment
that all the silent times between us
have gone

That the violet whispers have thinned
into lifeless air

Let's just be you and me
because nothing else matters

THE LIST

On a rainy day
you're feeling adventurous.
Grabbing a pen and notepad,
compose all the Tom, Dick, and Harrys.

You're doing great till
about number 13.
You aren't superstitious but
things start getting a little cloudy.

You begin to only remember faces
and even they get a little fuzzy.
I guess they don't count if they don't
have a face which is good news.

You can start all over with
A fresh clean slate.

I WILL CALL HER JACKIE

But that is not her real name

Oh Jackie
you are one shallow mess
Your nose is stuck so fAr up in the air
birds use it to perch on.

It's all about your cunt, as it should be
because your face is a train wreck.
You fake it so Much,
I almost feel sorry for your stupid ass.

They whisper behind your bAck,
*"Go after that one, she would wrap her legs
 around a telephone pole if it asked her to."*
Your ears must be riNging off
the receiver.

You must be a delectable Dish
but not because you taste so good.
You're so damn simple to pleAse.
I bet you coMe with a side of
dipping sauce between your thighs.

Boys like dirty sluts,
they're easY to bag up
and easy to spit out.

I have some advice for that
over stretched cavE you call a vagina.
You shouldn't steal
another girl's man.

She will wRite a poem

117

exposing your filthy little secret
and there'**S** nothing you can
do about it.

HIM

I wrote your name in the sand
hoping you would see it
from where you stand.

For just an instant you would know
I was thinking of you.
I'll crawl back into the corner
hoping you will follow.

We can share our secrets
when no one is looking.
It would be like that brief moment
in our history
when we were children
stealing each other's glance.

WHAT MOVES ME

The way smoke from a lit cigarette twists into different shapes in the air, the way your warm breath lingers on a window. The way night chases the dawn, or the way stars stare back at you on your long walk home after a night of tequila and ale. The smell of summer and the noise flip flops make when you walk. When a gust of wind blows a young girl's skirt up and you hear her laughter. The way a boy looks in the eyes of a beautiful woman and wants to touch her in dirty places. The sound rain drops make when they cover the ground in a blanket of wetness.

The way a kiss feels from a stranger or the way you feel after that first fuck. The hum of silence, the hum of noise, the static in your mind when it goes blank. Dreams that create confusion, lust, and fantasy. The nightmares of dying too young. The memories of loneliness and pain. The regrets that filter through your veins like wine. The way words cling to the page of a suicide note, the way the knife cuts the delicate skin of youth. The aroma of death, of birth. The stream of sweat running down your forehead from beating yourself off. It's all so fucking beautiful.

BECAUSE

Don't do it!
> *I have to*

Why?
> *Because*

Because why?
> *Because according to scientific studies*
> *there's no room for him here*

Insert gun smoke here

GIRLS HAVE A LOT TO THINK ABOUT

Girls have a lot
to think about these days

Sink or swim
Spit or swallow

There's only one thing
to remember in a tight situation

Don't bite off more
than you can chew

Because in most it's
a choking hazard

It would be one hell
of a way to go

FINAL SCENE

When the perfect moment arrives
I will make sure you will be
reading this at your weakest point.
It will be the last letter I will
ever write to you
under the influence of
bad music taste and intoxication.

I'm finding it difficult to
express any gratitude
toward you since the day
you stole my happy ending
but I however thank you
for wasting my time.
It has given me plenty to
think about along with extra loads
of laundry and dirty dishes.

There's a knock at the door.
Maybe it's my destiny coming to
save me from this nightmare of us
not getting anywhere.
Or maybe it's just the neighbor
asking to borrow some of that ego
that has attached itself to your shoulders.

I just want to say, "Fuck it all"
and buy that one way ticket
to anywhere that doesn't require
an emotional roller coaster.
The only thing stopping me is the distance
between me and the door.
What is it, 5 maybe 6 steps away?

Coming down from a high
we both sobered up from this fantasy
and realized we were bored.
If nothing was brought into this thing
nothing is what's coming out of it.

Like a bad movie
the end was coming before it began.
I fell silent when you asked
"In what direction are we headed?"
There is no "we".

There's only one way to end this thing.
One of us is going to have to grow
a set of balls and take matters into their own hands.
I just have to put one foot in front of the other.
Count the steps,

1

2

3

4

5

NOT AGAIN

You will not make me cry again,
my tears have seen their final days.

The oceans they have made
will disappear to the skies.

It's there you will find my kite flying
higher than the clouds.

CHASE A DREAM BEFORE IT FALLS

I can hardly keep holding on
Trying to chase a dream before it falls

I must be out of my mind
Doesn't seem real
The world around me
Is closing in

Can't get you out of my head
Tell me what I need
Tell me what it is I should seek
Give me a sign

Rescue me from these
Shadows swallowing me
I don't know how to keep breathing
On my own

Falling into a hole
That only you can fill
Reaching out in the hopes
You'll catch me before I crumble

Come set me free
From this place that's consuming me

I want to live again
Show me the way to turn

Hold me and tell me
You won't forget me when you're gone

WEEKEND GIRL

A healthy diet is very important
along with plenty of exercise.

Be sure to check expiration dates.
Packaged meat is only good for so long,

that's why she's a vegetarian 5 days
a week

DESIRE

She's a dirty little bitch

Someday you will know
but for now it's in my mind.

I can't talk about it
because they will find me
and bury me alive.

It will be quick like the way
lightening burns the sky.

I'm sharp like the thorn in
your boot.

I will sing until your ears pop,
my ghost will dance with your
skeleton key.

Dreams will become colossal,
my hands will speak in secret code.

I look past your eyes
because if I don't you will
see what I'm hiding in mine.

My mouth is a grotto,
come explore it with knives.

Hold my head underwater,
tell me to drink it like wine.

Take it all in, look around.
Remember what you see,

128

this is a love disease.

Take over the battlefield,
I'll wave the flag.

Tell me to drive fast,
tell me to power drive in the ground.

This will all be written on paper
somewhere.

You will have to find it before
they do, they won't understand.

I will climb high
so I can't be reached,
I can't be touched, even by me.

Night will settle in,
I suck burning ashes through
a straw.

Swim in white noise,
splash graffiti on the walls.

This is how you take it down,
take it all down,
one by one.

DEATH OF A SEASON

Stone faces
Weathered hands
Wandering in careless stride

Hearts made of ice
Frozen in angular glaciers
This season has grown into shadows

Pieces of the sun
Peeking through the window
Clinging to the walls

This mountain does not wake
This is the death of souls
And of you and I

SOMETHING KIND OF TRAGIC

I am a poet
that does what poets do best.
Writing about how much it hurts
or the one that got away.

Everything grows tired eventually.
Selling heartbreaks for fresh blood
isn't that fascinating when it's not yours.

I'm running out of ways to feel.
Maybe this is the end,
the dying verse.

I have nothing left to give
but these last tiny fragments
from the ink in my pen.

You have to become friends with death
if you want to make it out alive.
I will walk the tunnel with open arms.

Acknowledgements

First and foremost, my deepest love and gratitude goes to my little super heroes. They are the reason I get up every morning before 7:00 am, literally. They give me the strength to keep going even when the sun doesn't shine so high. Much appreciation goes out to my closest friend Andrea. I can't thank her enough for putting up with my craziness. She's also the best damn alibi a girl can have.

For those random strays that have wandered in and out of my life, you have opened my eyes to new writing material. I owe a lot to ex-lovers and secret crushes. I actually do have the ability to write a few good love poems so thank you for bringing out that side of me.

A special thank you goes out to my longtime friend Tina Foote for allowing me to share her incredible artwork between the pages.

List of Illustrations

All artwork courtesy of Tina Foote:

Pg. ix "Denial," acrylic on board, 30 x 40

Pg. 16 "All But Lost," acrylic on board, 30 x 40

Pg. 30 "Some Things Never Change," acrylic on board, 40 x 30

Pg. 61 "Sincerely," acrylic on board, 40 x 30

Pg. 72 "A Glorious Mess," acrylic on board, 30 x 40

Pg. 100 "Such a Long Way Down," acrylic on board, 40 x 30

Pg. 114 "No Regrets," acrylic on board, 40 x 30

Pg. 132 "The Turning Point," acrylic on board 30x40

Born and raised in a small town in upstate New York, Tina Foote found herself drawn to the beauty of art at a very young age. With no formal training, she learned from her mistakes and refined her ability. Over time she has found herself compelled to working with oil and pastel mediums. Today, Tina specializes in erotic and artistic nudes. Tina currently lives in Florida and continues to learn with each new painting. More about Tina's art and where to purchase can be found at www.fineartamerica.com.

Made in the USA
Charleston, SC
19 November 2012